servicenow

certified system administrator
handbook

Authors' Profile

Muhammad Zeeshan Ali
PMP, PMI-ACP, SA, CSA, OCP

Zeeshan is a prolific author with a wealth of experience spanning over 22 years in managing a diverse array of mid to large-scale projects across both Public and Private sectors. His expertise extends to various domains including Agile framework, Traditional Project Management, Performance Management, PMO, Leadership, Team Building, and Personal Motivation. He is renowned for pioneering the innovative "Performance Measurement Matrix," a groundbreaking tool for quantifying performance metrics for both individual software engineers and teams.

A staunch advocate for Agile methodologies, processes, and team skill enhancement, Zeeshan has demonstrated proficiency in managing multiple complex projects concurrently, often with teams dispersed across different geographical locations. He holds a Master's degree in Project Management, a Bachelor's degree in Computer Sciences, and is recognized as a Project Management Professional (PMP) and Agile Certified Professional (PMI-ACP) by the Project Management Institute (PMI), USA. Additionally, he is a Certified SAFe 6 Agilist (SA) by Scaled Agile and a Certified System Administrator (CSA) by ServiceNow.

Saqib Javed John
PMP, PMI-ACP, CSA, ITIL, SCJP, SCWCD, FIDIC

Saqib is one of the founding members and Managing Director of Organizational Governance Management Consultants (OGMC). He has professional expertise of more than 18 years of working on enterprise projects in various business domains ranging from a functional organization to project-based organization.

Saqib has immense experience in developing and managing human behavior, process engineering and optimization, risk management, conflict management, performance maturity audits and policy-making. This is one of the reasons he is relatable to readers of Business and management professions. He is best known for his rapid-learning techniques and easy methods of practical implementations. He also has contributed to many anthologies. His work is helping thousands of students, teachers and professionals.

Saqib is MS (IT), certified "Project Management Professional" (PMP) and "Agile Certified Practitioner" (ACP) from Project Management Institute (PMI) USA. He is also certified in "Information Technology Infrastructure Library" (ITIL) from Exin UK, "Sun Certified Java Programmer" (SCJP) and "Sun Certified Web Component Developer" (SCWCD) from Sun Microsystems USA.

servicenow
certified system administrator
handbook

Muhammad Zeeshan Ali
PMP, PMI-ACP, SA, CSA, OCP

Saqib Javed John
PMP, PMI-ACP, CSA, ITIL, SCJP, SCWCD

TECMAN

2024

Copyright © 2024 by TecMan Academy

All rights reserved. This book or any portion thereof may not be reproduced or used in any manner whatsoever without the express written permission of the copyright owner except for the use of brief quotations in a book review or scholarly journal.

Although the author and the publisher have made every effort to ensure the accuracy and completeness of information entered in this book, we assume no responsibility for errors, inaccuracies, omissions, or inconsistencies included herein. Any slights of people, places, or organizations are completely unintentional.

All inquiries should be addressed to (e-mail): publications@tecman.academy

First Printing: 2024

ISBN: 9798324555511

Ordering Information:

Special discounts are available on quantity purchases by corporations, associations, educators, and others. For details, contact the publisher at the above-listed address.

Dedicated to all the readers

and

those who inspired this work.

Preface

ServiceNow Certified System Administrator (CSA) Handbook is your roadmap to mastering the essential skills and knowledge required to excel as a ServiceNow Certified System Administrator.

In today's fast-paced digital environment, ServiceNow has emerged as a cornerstone platform for organizations seeking to streamline their operations, enhance efficiency, and deliver exceptional service experiences. As a ServiceNow CSA, you play a vital role in harnessing the full potential of this platform to drive innovation and deliver value to your organization.

This book is carefully curated to provide you with a structured framework for navigating the diverse facets of ServiceNow administration. Each section of the outline is meticulously crafted to cover key topics, from foundational concepts to advanced techniques, ensuring comprehensive coverage of the CSA exam blueprint.

Whether you are preparing for the CSA exam or seeking to enhance your expertise in ServiceNow administration, this outline serves as your guidebook, offering clarity, direction, and insight into the core competencies required for success in this role.

Drawing upon the collective wisdom of ServiceNow experts and practitioners, this outline distills years of industry experience into a concise and accessible format, designed to empower you with the knowledge and skills needed to excel as a ServiceNow CSA.

Whether you are embarking on your journey to become certified or looking to elevate your career to new heights, this book is your indispensable companion on the path to ServiceNow excellence. Dive in, explore, and embark on a transformative journey toward becoming a proficient and certified ServiceNow System Administrator.

About TecMan

TecMan Academy operates under the umbrella of OGMC (Organizational Governance Management Consultants). As specialists in ServiceNow, we offer a comprehensive range of expertise including Technical Consulting, Product Training, Implementation, and Application Administration. Our aim is to empower your organization with cutting-edge solutions, modernizing operations and fostering innovation throughout your entire IT infrastructure via a contemporary cloud-based platform.

Executing a successful transformation requires meticulous planning, administration, and setup. We deliver a holistic approach, supplying the necessary expertise, processes, and tools to streamline and automate your digital workflows and business operations.

Understanding the paramount importance of efficiency, our consultants leverage predictive intelligence to ensure timely and cost-effective implementation of solutions tailored to your specific requirements.

Visit our websites for more information:

ogmcs.com

tecman.academy

x

Table of Contents

1. ServiceNow Overview 1
2. User Interface 3
3. Roles & Rights Management 7
4. List & Filters 9
5. Forms 11
6. Data Structure 13
7. ACLs 15
8. Data Imports 17
9. Workflows 19
10. Flows 21
11. Notifications 23
12. Update Sets 25
13. Reporting 27
14. Dashboard 29
15. Knowledge Management 31
16. Service Catalog 35
17. Incident Management 39
18. Change Management 41
19. Problem Management 43

20.	SLA	45
21.	Instance Management	47
22.	Applications & Plugins	49
23.	System Properties	51
24.	Scripting	53
25.	Service Portal	55
26.	Widgets	57
27.	App Engine Studio	59
28.	Workspace	61
29.	Domain Separation	63
30.	API's	65
31.	Integration Methods	67
32.	Authentication Methods	69
33.	Case Management (HRSD)	73
34.	HRSD Performance Analytics	75
35.	Employ Service Center (ESC)	77
36.	Event Management	79
37.	Asset Management with CMDB	81
38.	Discovery	83
39.	MID Server & ECC Queue	85
40.	Customer Service Management (CSM)	87

41.	Virtual Agent	91
42.	Troubleshooting & Debugging	93
43.	ATFs	95
44.	Strategic Portfolio Management (SPM)	97
45.	SecOps	99
46.	Portals	101
47.	UI Policy	103
48.	UI Actions	105
49.	Business Rules	107
50.	Data Policy	109
Glossary		111

1. ServiceNow Overview

Why ServiceNow?

- Customization and Flexibility
- Seamless Integrations
- Cognitive AI Capabilities
- Robust Security
- Community Support
- Continual Service Improvement

ServiceNow Benefits:

- Streamlined Scalability & Workflows
- Improved Service Delivery
- Risk Mitigation
- Lower Operational Costs
- Real-Time Analytics & Dashboards

ServiceNow Platform:

- Application Platform as a Service (aPaaS)
- Enterprise Level Utilization
- AI & Automation
- Out of the Box (ITIL) Processes
- Well Integrated
- Successful Governance Model

ServiceNow Overview

ServiceNow Architecture:
- Cloud Based Computing Model
- Multi Instance Layers
- Single Data Design
- Highly Available Data Centers
- Frequent Backups

Supported Browsers:
- Chrome
- Microsoft Edge
- Firefox
- Apple Safari

2. User Interface

UI Navigation:

- Applications & Modules
- Favorites'
- History
- Workspaces
- Contextual App Pill
- Global Search
- Global Icon
- Sidebar Discussions
- Show Help
- Show Notifications
- User Menu (Profiles, Preferences, Impersonate User, Elevate Role)

Ways to Interact:

- Native UI (Next Experience Unified Navigation)
- Mobile Interface
- Portal Interface
- Agent Workspace
- Now Learning Platform
- ServiceNow Community
- ServiceNow Global Events
- ServiceNow Developer Site

User Interface

Core UI Components:
- Banner Frame
- Content Frame
- Application Navigator

Common UI Elements:
- Filters (Operators/Conditions)
- UI Actions/Button
- List Controls
- Tree Picker
- List Collector
- Activity Streams
- Condition Builder
- Manage Attachments

Branding Overview:
- Page Header (Caption, Background Color, Divider Stripe)
- Navigation (Header/Footer, sidebars, favorite icons, Background Color, Background expand Items, Separator Color, Unselected navigation tab icon)
- Tab (Icon Color, Background Color, Divider Bar, Browser Tab Title)
- Module Text Color
- Banner (Image & Text Color)
- Border Color

- Base Theme
- Date/Time Format (System Time Zone

User Interface

3. Roles & Rights Management

What is a User?

- User Module
- User Identification
- User Creation (Form & Fields)
- Unique Details
- Define Access
- User Table

Groups:

- Group Module
- Group Identification
- Group Creation (Group Form & Fields)
- Group Table & Related List
- Perform different Tasks

Roles:

- Role Module
- Role Identification
- Role Creation (Form & Fields)
- Control Access
- Role Table & Related List
- Different Roles
- Default Captures in Update set

Roles & Rights Management

User, Group & Role Mapping:

- Assign Role to User
- User & Role Link Table
- Assign Role to the Group
- Group & Role Link Table
- Add a User to group
- User & Group Link Table

User Access Management

- Inherited Roles
- Impersonate a User
- Elevate Role

4. List & Filters

List:
- Records of Table
- Rows & Columns
- Record & Fields
- List Characteristics (Searchable, Sortable, Editable)

List Elements:
- Title Bar
- Gear Icon
- List Control
- List Context Menu
- Filters
- Breadcrumbs

List Control:
- Views
- Filters
- Group By
- Show
- Create Favorite

List & Filters

List Context Menu:

- Sorting
- Show Visual Task Board
- Group/Ungroup
- Bar/Pie Chart
- Configure
- Import/Export

Filters:

- Set of Conditions
- Field
- Operator
- Value
- Connectors

5. Forms

Forms:
- Structured Layout
- One Record Information
- Specific Information
- View and Edit Records

Form Elements:
- Form Title
- Form Menu
- UI Actions
- Fields
- Sections
- Related List

Form Menu:
- Configure
- Export
- Views
- Favorite
- Reload Form

Forms

Form Layout:
- Configure Appearance of form
- Slush Bucket
- Show/Hide Fields on Form
- Create View
- Create Section
- Create Fields

Form Design:
- Graphical Tool
- Drag & Drop Interface
- Access Field Properties
- Parts of Form Design UI

6. Data Structure

Table & Fields:

- Tables
- Records
- List
- Data Related Tables

Tables:

- Collection of Records
- Rows
- Columns
- Sys_id

Fields:

- Types
- Field Name
- Field Label
- Field Value

Table Relationships:

- One to Many
- Many to Many
- Extended

Data Structure

Types of Tables:
- Base Tables
- Extended Tables
- Core Tables
- Custom Tables
- Schema Map

7. ACLs

Access Categories:

- What is ACL?
- Types of Permission
- Different level of Securities
- Login
- Visibility of Applications
- Tables & Records

Operation Restriction:

- Create
- Read
- Write
- Delete
- Execute
- Edit_task_relations
- save_as_template
- add_to_list
- list_edit
- report_on
- report_view
- personalize_choices

ACLs

ACL Form & Fields:
- Type
- Operation
- Admin Override
- Name of Table/ Object
- Required Role
- Condition
- Custom Condition

ACL Rule Types:
- Particular Element Configure for Security
- Table.None
- Table.*
- Table. Field

8. Data Imports

Ways of Data Imports:

- Import XML
- Import Excel
- Import Sets

Import Sets Components:

- Data Source
- Import Set Table
- Transform Map
- Mapping Assist
- Coalesce
- Target Table

Data Import Process:

- Load Data
- Create Transform Map
- Run Transform Map
- Check Data Integrity

Coalescing:

- Handle Collision
- Avoid Record Duplication
- Record Overwriting

Data Imports

Import Data Policy:

- Enforce Data Consistency
- Applies to data entered in a form
- Only make fields Mandatory & Read Only
- Runs on Server Side
- Cannot Apply Scripts

9. Workflows

What is Workflow?

- Automated Sequence of Activities
- Supports Repeatable steps/Actions
- Perform Activities as per it is defined in sequence
- Baseline Workflow

Workflow Lifecycle:

- Trigger Conditions
- Sequence of Activities & Actions
- Activity's conditions
- End of Workflow

Components of Workflow Editor:

- Canvas
- Canvas Tab
- Title Bar
- Palette
- Palette Tabs

Workflow activities:

- Approvals
- Conditions
- Notifications

Workflows

- On Call
- Service Catalog
- Subflows
- Tasks
- Timers
- Utilities

Activities with Scripting:
- Approval User
- Approval Group
- If
- Wait for Condition
- Notification
- Create Event
- Run Script
- Rest Message

10. Flows

Flows

- Automating Process
- Triggers & Actions
- Use Natural Language
- Integrate with external systems

Flow Designer Components:

- Flow
- Subflows
- Actions
- Core Actions
- Action Steps
- Spokes

Flow Trigger Types:

- Record is Created
- Record is Updated
- Record is Created or Updated
- On a Particular Schedule
- Applications Specific Conditions are met
- Inbound Email

Flows

Process:

- Flow is Triggered
- Process Event Queue
- Build Process Plan
- Run Process Plan
- Store Flow Execution

States:

- Waiting
- In Progress
- Error
- Cancelled
- Completed

11. Notifications

What are Notifications?

- Messages or Alerts
- Notifies Users or Groups
- Enhances communication

Inbound/Outbound:

- Outbound Notification
- Inbound Action
- To trigger actions or updates

Applications:

- Email
- Digest Interval
- Notification
- Notification Email Script
- Notification Categories
- Templates
- Notification Filters
- Email Access Restriction
- Push
- Provider

Notifications

Notification Form:
- Name
- Table
- Category
- When to Send
- Who will Receive
- What it will Contain

Inbound Action Form:
- Name
- Target Table
- Action Type
- Stop Processing
- When to Run
- Action
- Description

12. Update Sets

What is an Update Set?
- Group of Configuration Changes
- Moved From one Instance to Another
- Group Series of Changes
- Move as a Unit

Items Captured by Default:
- Form Configurations
- UI Policies
- Business Rules
- Client Scripts
- UI Actions
- Script Includes ...etc

Items Not Captured by Default:
- CMDB Records
- Users
- Groups
- Scheduled Jobs
- System Properties ...etc

Update Sets

Planning Process:

- Same Version Instance
- Correct Update set Selection
- Instance Cloned
- Movement Path
- Clear Naming Conventions
- Preview & Commit
- Review before Moving
- Update Set Backup
- Manage Conflicts

Move Update Sets Among Instances:

- Dev
- UAT
- Staging
- Prod

13. Reporting

Introduction:
- Identifying Trends
- Monitoring Field Values
- Looking for Outlying Data
- Tracking Work
- Viewing Progress

Types:
- Bars
- Pies & Donuts
- Time Series
- Multidimensional Reports
- Scores
- Other

Report Designer:
- Data
- Type
- Configure
- Style

Reporting

Datasets in Reports:
- Display Report of up to 5 Tables
- Group By Limitations
- Bar
- Horizontal Bar
- Column
- Line
- Step Line
- Area
- Spline

Sharing:
- Share
- Schedule
- Add to Dashboard
- Export to PDF

14. Dashboard

Introduction:

- Drag & Drop Canvas
- Gathering Visualization
- Widgets
- Interactive Filters

Creating Dashboard:

- Name
- Group
- Order
- Restrict to Roles
- Owner

Adding Widgets:

- Using Widget Picker
- Configure Widgets
- Background Color
- Increase/Decrease Height
- Edit
- Refresh Widget

Tabs:

- Organizing Widgets
- Logical Grouping
- Create
- Edit
- Delete

Interactive Filters:

- Filter Reports without Modifying
- Filters the Data in Reports
- Types of Interactive Filters
- Add as a Widget

15. Knowledge Management

Overview:

- Managing Information
- Sharing Information
- Supports processes
- Knowledge Bases
- Articles

Process Flow:

- Creation of Article
- Review
- Published
- Retired

Plugins:

- Knowledge Management Core
- Knowledge Management Advanced Installer
- Knowledge Management Advanced
- Predictive Intelligence for Knowledge Management
- Performance Analytics - Content Pack - Knowledge Management
- Knowledge Management V3
- I18N: Knowledge Management Internationalization Plugin v2
- Knowledge Document

Knowledge Management

- Knowledge Management - External Content Integration
- Knowledge Management Wiki Support
- Knowledge Management KCS Capabilities
- Knowledge Management - Add-in for Microsoft Word
- Knowledge Blocks
- Knowledge Overview

Knowledge Homepage:
- Organize Articles
- Categories
- Search & Read Article
- Create an article
- Post a Question

Versioning:
- Maintain Multiple Versions
- Enable Article Versioning
- Recall Button
- Checkout Button
- List of Versions
- Outdated

Article States:
- Draft
- Review

- Scheduled for Publish
- Published
- Pending Retirement
- Retired
- Outdated

16. Service Catalog

Overview:

- Self Service
- Catalog Items
- Service/Product
- Service Portal
- User Friendly Interface

Terms & Roles:

- Execution Plans
- Execution Plan Tasks
- Fulfilment Groups
- Tickets
- Administrator [admin]
- Catalog administrator [catalog_admin]
- Catalog manager [catalog_manager]
- Catalog editor [catalog_editor]
- Catalog builder editor [catalog_builder_editor]

Types:

- Standard Catalog Item
- Record Producer
- Order Guide
- Content Item

Service Catalog

Catalog Item Form:
- Name
- Catalog
- Category
- Item Details
- Process Engine
- Picture
- Pricing
- Portal Setting
- Variables
- Variable Sets
- UI Policies
- Client Scripts

Variables & Types:
- Specify questions for a Catalog Item
- Break
- Check box
- Container (Start, Split, End)
- Date
- Date and time
- Duration
- Email
- HTML
- IP Address

- Label
- List collector
- Lookup multiple choice
- Lookup select box
- Custom
- Custom with label
- Masked
- Multi-line text
- Multiple choice
- Numeric scale
- Reference
- Requested For
- Rich Text Label
- Select box
- Single-line text
- UI page
- URL
- Wide single-line text
- Yes/No
- Attachment

Service Catalog

17. Incident Management

Overview:

- Incident
- Reporting Issue
- Define Priority
- Assignment
- Escalation
- Resolve

Incident Process:

- User Submits an Incident
- Incident Assigned to the Group
- Agents Start working
- Incident Resolved

Incident Modules:

- Create New
- Assigned to Me
- Open
- Open – Unassigned
- Resolved
- All
- Overview
- Critical Incidents Map

Incident Management

States:
- New
- In Progress
- On Hold
- Resolved
- Closed

Lifecycle:
- Investigation
- Promotion
- Escalation
- Resolve

18. Change Management

Overview:
- Change
- Systematic Approach
- Control Changes
- Minimize Risk
- Minimize Impact

Lifecycle:
- Create Change Request
- Review Change
- Change Evaluation
- Change Approvals
- Implementation
- Validation

Types:
- Standard
- Emergency
- Normal

Change Management

States:

- New
- Assess
- Authorize
- Scheduled
- Implement
- Review
- Closed
- Cancelled

Change Creation:

- New From Change Module
- From a CI
- Standard Change Catalog
- Copy an Existing Change

19. Problem Management

Overview:
- Problem
- Manage Issues
- Identify Problem
- Resolve Problem
- Identify root cause of Service Affecting Problems

Lifecycle:
- Problem Detection
- Categorize and Prioritize
- Investigate and Diagnose
- Resolve and close the problem
- Major problem review

Benefits:
- Continuous service improvement
- Avoid Costly Incidents
- Increased Productivity
- Decreased Time to Resolution
- Speed up service restoration
- Minimize service disruptions
- Accelerate root cause resolution

Problem Management

Problem Modules:

- Create New
- Assigned to Me
- Known Errors
- Open
- Pending
- All
- Overview

States:

- Open
- Pending Change
- Known Error
- Closed
- Resolved

20. SLA

Overview:

- Contract
- Specific Targets and Metrics
- Duration of Completion of Task
- Response Time
- Resolution Time

SLA Definition Form:

- Name
- Type
- Target
- Table
- Flow
- Duration
- Schedule
- Time zone
- Start Condition
- Pause Condition
- Stop Condition
- Reset Condition

SLA

Benefits:
- Improved customer experience
- Improved employee experience
- Established and trusted source of information
- Increased productivity and performance

Duration & Schedule:
- Relative Duration
- User Specified Duration
- No Schedule
- SLA Definition
- Table Field

Time Zone:
- The Caller's Time Zone
- SLA Definition Time Zone
- CI's Location's Time Zone
- Task's Location's Time Zone
- Caller's Location's Time Zone

21. Instance Management

Instance Upgrade:

- New ServiceNow release version
- New Functionality
- Two Major Releases Each Year
- Improves platform performance

Upgrade Process:

- Plan
- Prepare
- Schedule Upgrade
- Review Upgrade
- Test & Validate
- Remediate
- Production Upgrade

Instance Cloning:

- Request Clone
- Copy instance
- Copy Data
- Nightly Backup

Instance Management

Cloning Process:

- Login to Instance you want to Clone
- Create a Clone Target
- Add or Remove tables to Exclude
- Data Preservers
- Preserve any unpublished applications
- Request Clone
- Clone profiles for clone requests
- Select the target instance
- Clone Scheduled Start Time
- Email upon completion

Best Practices:

- Backup Data
- Plan Thoroughly
- Clone Environment
- Review Customizations
- Test in Sandbox
- Communicate Changes
- Monitor and Troubleshoot
- Document Changes
- Perform Post-Upgrade Validation

22. Applications & Plugins

Difference between Plugins & Applications:

- Application is a standalone piece of code
- Installed & Used on Platform
- Mini Program
- Application implements a collection of features
- Plugin is not standalone
- Plugin provides feature enhancements to installed applications
- Adds extra features

Activate Plugins:

- Some are By Default Activated
- activate additional plugins on your instance
- Other plugins require activation
- Some Require Subscription

Request a Plugin:

- Plugin not available on App Page
- Request Activation
- Activate Plugin page
- All Applications page

Applications & Plugins

Mobile Plugins (Core):

- Mobile App Builder
- Mobile App Builder API
- Mobile Card Builder
- ServiceNow Now Mobile app screens and launcher screens
- Human Resources Scoped App: Mobile

Supporting plugins (Mobile)

- SG Offline support
- Service Management Geolocation
- Geolocation
- Glide Virtual Agent

23. System Properties

Overview:

- Configuration information
- Control the system behavior
- Instead of Fix Values
- System properties table

Available system properties:

- cdu.record.watcher.timeout
- com.cmdb.baseline.max_changes
- com.glide.cs.collab.event_queue.enabled
- com.glide.cs.collab.event_queue.threshold
- com.glide.cs.collab.teams_outage_timer
- com.glide.cs.conversation_history_cross_channel.enabled

Add a system property:

- Navigate to sys_properties.list
- Verify Existence
- New
- Fill form
- Submit

System Properties

Create a system properties module:

- Navigate Application Menu
- Search Application
- Click New
- Submit
- Verify Module Creation

Create a System Properties Category:

- Create Application File
- System Property Category
- Configure New File
- Save

24. Scripting

Overview:

- Beyond Standard Configurations
- Addition to OOB Functionality
- Automate Processes
- Add Functionality
- Integrate
- APIs
- Glide Classes

Client-Side Scripting:

- Runs on Client Side
- Appearance of forms
- Display Fields
- onLoad
- onChange
- onSubmit

Client-side Glide Classes:

- GlideAjax
- GlideDialogWindow
- GlideForm
- GlideList2
- GlideMenu

Scripting

- GlideUser

Server-Side Scripting:

- Database Operations
- Server Side
- Records are Accessed
- Modified

Server-side Glide classes:

- GlideRecord
- GlideElement
- GlideSystem
- GlideAggregate
- GlideDateTime

25. Service Portal

Overview:

- User Friendly Interface
- Centralised Hub
- Request Services/Resources
- Extensively Customizable
- Easily Accessible

Frameworks:

- HTML
- CSS
- JavaScript
- Bootstrap
- Angular JS

Service Portals:

- Employee Center
- Service Portal
- Anonymous Report Center
- Knowledge Portal

Service Portal

Anatomy:

- URL or a Module
- Pages
- Containers
- Widgets

Configuration:

- Branding Editor
- Designer
- Page Editor
- Widget Editor
- New Portal
- Get Help

26. Widgets

Overview:

- Defines Content
- Reusable Components
- Consist of HTML, CSS, Client Side, Server-Side Code
- Baseline Widgets
- Custom Widgets

Adding Widgets to Page:

- Containers
- Drag & Drop
- Valid Location
- Columns

Widget Instance:

- Widget Instance
- Location
- Properties
- CSS
- Multiple Instances

Widgets

Service Catalog Widgets:

- To Build a Catalog
- Plugins
- Catalog Content widget
- Catalog Homepage Search widget

Configure:

- Configurable
- Service Portal Designer
- point to the Edit icon
- control + right-click menu

27. App Engine Studio

Overview:

- Guided Local Tool
- Low Code Tool
- Automate Business Process
- Templates

Tools:

- UI Builder
- Catalog Builder
- Mobile App Builder
- Flow Designer
- Table Builder

Pillars:

- Data
- Experience
- Automation
- Security

Phases:

- Panning
- Developing
- Testing & Debugging

App Engine Studio

- Deployment
- Maintenance

Applications Scope:
- Scoped Applications
- Uniquely Identifies
- Protection
- Availability
- Configuration

28. Workspace

Overview:

- Single-pane view
- Suite of Tools
- Tabbed Format
- Targeted Experience
- Data Visualizations

Agent Views:

- Landing Page
- List view
- Record view
- Agent Chat

Key features:

- Single-pane view
- Integrated communication channels
- Integrated email client
- Agent assistance
- Playbook
- Reorder Workspace Tabs

Workspace

Types:
- CMDB Workspace
- Agent Workspace for HR Service Delivery
- Agent Workspace for Request Management
- Customer Service Management Agent Workspace
- Dispatcher Workspace
- Field Service in CSM Agent Workspace
- IT Service Management Agent Workspace
- Service Owner Workspace
- Survey Designer
- Vendor Manager Agent Workspace
- Workforce Optimization for Customer Service
- Workforce Optimization for ITSM

Benefits:
- Increase productivity
- Deliver engaging experiences
- Work smart, work fast
- Build quickly

29. Domain Separation

Overview:

- Sub-Tenant Platform Architecture
- Logical groupings
- Data Segregation
- Managed Service Providers (MSPs)
- Data Visibility

Pros:

- Volume licensing
- Centralized administration of customers as tenants
- Data segregation
- Global reporting
- Upgradability and scalability
- Lower minimum license threshold
- Pre-built processes and capabilities
- Reduced staff requirements
- Faster on-boarding
- Shared instance costs
- Services offered by the provider

Cons:

- Data isn't truly separate
- Admin control stays with the Service Provider

Domain Separation

- Adding new services will be harder
- It can only be enabled in a new instance

When to Use?
- Logical data separation
- Scale
- Platform requirements
- Process differences
- Administration requirements

Plugin:
- Domain Separation
- Domain Table
- Separate policy
- Global domain
- Determines the domain

30. API's

Client API:

- DynamicTranslation – Client
- g_service_catalog – Client
- GlideAjax – Client
- GlideDocument – Client
- GlideForm – Client
- GlideRecord – Client

Client mobile API:

- cabrillo.attachments – Client
- cabrillo.camera – Client
- cabrillo.navigation – Client
- cabrillo.nowapp – Client
- cabrillo.viewLayout – Client
- cabrillo.message – Client

Server Scoped API:

- AgentNowHandler – Scoped
- AuthCredential – Scoped
- CatalogJS – Scoped
- CatalogItemVariable – Scoped
- CatCategory – Scoped
- CatItem – Scoped

API's

Server Global API:

- GlideDate – Global
- GlideDateTime – Global
- GlideElement – Global
- Event – Global
- GlideConversation – Global
- GlideUser – Global

Rest API:

- Account API
- Agent Client Collector API
- Aggregate API
- Batch API
- Case API
- Contact API

31. Integration Methods

REST (Inbound):

- Representational State Transfer
- Easy Communication
- Supported HTTP request methods
- Data format headers
- REST API ACLs

Scripted REST APIs (Inbound):

- Custom web service APIs
- Scripts to manage
- Request and response formats
- Scripted REST API security
- Scripted REST API access controls

SOAP (Inbound):

- Simple Object Access Protocol (SOAP)
- Web service provider
- WSDL
- Long-running SOAP request support
- Timeout protection

Integration Methods

SOUP (Outbound):

- Outbound SOAP messages
- SOAP message
- Connectivity details
- Outbound SOAP security
- Scripting outbound SOAP

REST (Outbound):

- REST message elements
- Outbound REST authentication
- Variable substitution
- Scripting outbound REST

32. Authentication Methods

Multi-Provider Single sign-on (SSO):

- Identity Providers (IdPs)
- Configuring users
- Configuring properties
- Properties
- Plugins

OAuth Inbound and Outbound authentication:

- Authentication protocol
- OAuth 2.0
- Access tokens
- Inbound
- Outbound

API access policy:

- Duration of access
- Plugins
- custom API access policy
- access policy

Digest token authentication:

- HTTP header value
- Hash value

Authentication Methods

- More secure
- Requirements

Time limited authentication:
- Expiry time
- fetch nonce
- existing channel
- low privileged roles

Multi-Factor Authentication:
- second level of authentication
- passcode
- hardware key
- biometric authenticator
- SMS or Email

Self-register:
- Identity verification
- Commonly used registration flows.
- self-registration
- configure the registration

LDAP:
- Integrate
- Streamline Login Process

- Features
- LDAP user record updates

Authentication Methods

33. Case Management (HRSD)

Overview:
- Assists HR personnel
- Employee Submitted Queries
- HR workflows
- Centralized Dashboard
- Self-service portals

Plugins:
- Human Resources Scoped App: Security
- Human Resources Scoped App: Integrations
- Document Templates
- Human Resources Scoped App: Mobile

HR Services:
- Requests and Assistance
- HR request to fulfilment process
- HR service configuration
- HR service catalog management
- HR template configuration

Case Lifecycle:
- Initiation
- Intake and Categorization

Case Management (HRSD)

- Assignment and Prioritization
- Investigation and Collaboration
- Resolution
- Closure
- Feedback and Continuous Improvement

Case Transfer & Escalation:
- Transfer an HR Case
- Methods
- Escalate an HR Case
- Why to Escalate?

34. HRSD Performance Analytics

Overview:
- Collecting & Analyzing Data
- Key performance indicators
- Actionable Insights
- Up-to-date visualizations

Reporting vs Analytics:
- Reporting shows current state
- Data as discrete facts
- Reporting doesn't predict future
- Analytics shows trends
- Relationships between data sets
- Analytics predict future outcomes

Premium Plugin:
- Performance Analytics - Premium
- Limitations
- License is required
- Custom applications Requirement
- Features

HRSD Performance Analytics

Architecture:
- Data Collectors
- Indicator Sources
- Indicators
- Breakdown Sources
- Breakdowns

HR analytics in practice:
- Collecting data
- Measurement
- Analysis
- Application

35. Employ Service Center (ESC)

Overview:

- Unified portal experience
- Extensible service delivery platform
- Available to all customers
- Employee engagement and communication

Key Attributes:

- Easily scalable
- Customizable
- Unified browse
- Automate Processes
- Employee-centric approach

Plugins:

- Employee center core
- Employee Center
- Employee Center Pro
- Employee Experience Taxonomy
- Employee Experience Foundation
- Content Experiences:
- Content Publishing
- Employee Profile

Employ Service Center (ESC)

Employee Center and Employee Center Pro:
- Pre-Installed Application
- Licensed Application
- Separately Installed
- Homepages
- Comparison

Functionalities:
- Curated Experiences
- Unified browse
- Content Experiences widget
- App Launcher
- Tasks and approvals
- Content Experiences widget (Employee Center Pro)
- Integration-powered capabilities (Employee Center Pro)
- Content Publishing (Employee Center Pro)
- Enterprise search (Employee Center Pro)
- Employee Forums (Employee Center Pro)

36. Event Management

What is Event Management?

- Monitor Health
- Event and alert analysis
- MID Server
- Service is affected by an event

What Event Management can manage?

- Discovered services
- Application services
- Dynamic CI groups
- Alert groups

Structure:

- Event Occurs
- Event Sends to the Instance
- Generate Alerts
- Applies alert management rules

Workflow:

- Receives external events
- Generates alerts
- Events are sent to instance
- MID Server sends information

Event Management

- Event Table

Event Management and Service Mapping:

- Discovered services
- Automated alert groups
- Locates CI information
- CI stored in CMDB

37. Asset Management with CMDB

Understanding CMDB and its Architecture:

- Create/Maintain logical configurations
- Mapping
- Configuration Items (CI)
- Dependencies
- Relationships

Categorizing Assets:

- Class
- Model Category
- Model
- Unique Assets

Asset Management Goals:

- Control inventory
- Reduce Cost
- Tools
- Compliance
- Create standards

Asset Management with CMDB

Asset Management Life Cycle:
- Request
- Procure
- Receive
- Stock
- Deploy
- Support
- Maintain
- Retired

38. Discovery

Overview:
- Finds Devices
- Update CIs
- Horizontal Discovery
- Top-down discovery
- Service Mapping

Components to find CIs:
- Probes
- Sensors
- Patterns

Phases:
- Scanning
- Classification
- Identification
- Exploration

Communication through MID Server:
- Queries the instance
- Communicate using SOAP on HTTP
- Agentless
- Simple Network Management Protocol (SNMP)

Discovery

Types of discovery:

- Network discovery
- CI discovery
- Cloud discovery
- Server less discovery

39. MID Server & ECC Queue

What is MID Server?

- Java application
- Runs on Server
- Control and Secure
- Communication with external Apps

Application:

- Instructions
- Downloads
- Dashboard
- Servers
- Server Issues
- Upgrade History
- Clusters

ECC Queue:

- External Communication Channel
- Information Sent form ServiceNow
- Information receives from another system
- Input
- Output

MID Server & ECC Queue

ECC Queue Flow:

- New Message creates
- Check for Input or Output
- State is Ready
- Sends Job to MID Server
- State is Processing

MID Server uses ECC Queue:

- AMB Notifies MID Server
- ECC Queue sets status, if Job available
- MID Server does the work
- MID Server Reports back o ECC Queue

40. Customer Service Management (CSM)

Overview:
- Support to External Customer
- Resolve Issues
- Customer Satisfaction
- Automation

Features:
- Self- Service
- Order Management
- Optimization
- Omni channel
- Intelligence
- Install Base management
- Engagement Messenger for CSM
- Customer Data Management
- Case management
- Analytics and Insights
- Agent experience

Plugins:
- Agent Workspace
- Assessment

Customer Service Management (CSM)

- Asset Management
- Assignment Workbench
- Customer Service Base Extension Entities
- Customer Service Portal
- Customer Service Social Integration
- Customer Service Spoke
- Glide Conversation Server
- Openframe
- Process Flow Formatter
- Resource Matching Engine
- Skills Management
- Special Handling Notes
- State Flows
- Subscriptions and Activity Feed Framework
- Task Activities
- Task Relations
- Virtual Agent Service Portal Widgets

Order Management:
- Order Products
- Update Orders
- Order Status
- Set Up Product

Order Management Benefits:

- Cloud- Based Order System
- Data model
- CSM Agent Workspace
- Configurable product offerings
- User-friendly Portal

41. Virtual Agent

Overview:

- Chatbot
- User Assistance
- Automated Conversations
- Solve Ordinary Issues
- Elevated user experience

Components:

- Virtual Agent conversational (client) interface
- Virtual Agent Designer
- Live agent support
- Large language models (LLM) support

Plugins:

- Conversational Analytics
- Integration - Multiple Provider Single Sign-On Installer
- Localization Framework Installer
- NLU Model for Virtual Agent Setup Topics
- Proxy Agent to the ServiceNow Natural Language Understanding Server
- Proxy Agent to the IBM Watson Natural Language Understanding server
- Proxy Agent to the Microsoft LUIS Natural Language Understanding server

Virtual Agent

- Proxy Agent to the Google Dialog flow ES Natural Language Understanding server
- Topic Recommendations
- Virtual Agent integration with actionable notifications

Features:
- Personalized experiences
- Now Assist in Virtual Agent
- Natural Language Understanding (NLU)
- Pre-built conversational topics
- Virtual Agent Designer
- Live agent hand-off
- NLU Workbench
- Channel integrations
- Notifications
- Multiple NLU providers

Designer:
- Diagram tool
- Design topics
- Topics page
- Topic properties
- Topic flow

42. Troubleshooting & Debugging

Debugging:
- System Processes
- Debugging Features
- Console Log
- Test script inaccuracy
- Invalid Test Data

Script Debugger:
- Debug Server-Side Scripts
- Step through code line-by-line
- View the values of local, global, and private variables
- Debugger Components

ACL Debugger:
- Troubleshot ACLs
- Debug ACLs
- Field level debugging
- ACL rule output messages

Debug Business Rules:
- Script Editor
- Looks for error
- Verification

Troubleshooting & Debugging

- System Logs

Technical Best Practices:

- Make Code Easy to Read
- Create Small, Modular Components
- Variables
- Interacting with the Database
- Use Self-Executing Functions
- Avoid Coding Pitfalls

43. ATFs

Overview:
- Automate Testing
- Execution of Tests
- Test driven development
- Regression testing
- Regular checkups
- Uses

Benefits:
- Replaces Manual Testing
- Reusable Test Cases
- Reduces human errors
- Quality of client deliverables
- Accelerate Testing Process

Components:
- Test
- Test Suite
- Quick Start Test
- Test Steps
- Step Configuration
- Input/output
- Test Result

ATFs

- Step Result
- Assert

What we can Test?
- Service Catalog in Service Portal
- Application Navigator
- Custom UI
- Form
- Service Catalog
- Forms in Service Portal
- REST
- Server

Parallel Testing:
- Running multiple tests
- Avoiding resource conflicts
- Parallel testing limit
- Test waiting queue

44. Strategic Portfolio Management (SPM)

Overview:
- Processes and Tools
- Align work to strategy
- Resource Allocation
- Business Decision
- Compiling and maintaining the right investments

Benefits:
- Faster time to market
- Improved response time to disruptions
- Better alignment between strategy and execution
- Improved efficiency
- Cohesion of multiple disciplines
- Increased agility
- Improved speed overall

Process:
- Inventory
- Analysis
- Planning
- Execution

Strategic Portfolio Management (SPM)

SPM Use Cases:

- Capital planning
- Dynamic planning
- Enterprise program and portfolio management
- IT strategic planning
- Strategy Execution Management

Plugins:

- Service Portfolio Management Core
- Service Catalog core applications
- Report Engine- use summary table for report
- Service Portfolio Management SLA Commitments
- Service Portfolio Management Taxonomy Content Pack

45. SecOps

Overview:

- Security Tools
- Collaboration between IT security and IT operations
- IT performance
- Resolve Threats

Steps:

- Establish
- Integrate
- Prioritize
- Utilize
- Informed & Govern
- Automate
- Visualize

Basic Components:

- Earlier detection and prioritization
- Increased transparency
- Security improvements
- Threat awareness

What does a SecOps center do?

- Continuous network monitoring
- Incident response
- Forensics and root cause analysis
- Threat intelligence

Benefits:

- Return on investment
- Security and operations become streamlined
- Reduced resources
- Fewer cloud security issues
- Fewer app disruptions
- Better auditing procedures

46. Portals

What is a portal?
- ServiceNow user interface (UI)
- Access any platform component
- Access Platform Features
- Configurable

Portal Anatomy:
- URL/Module
- Pages
- Containers
- Widgets

Explore a Portal:
- Open a Portal
- Explore
- Visit Different Pages
- Request Something
- Submit

Configuration:
- Branding Editor
- Designer
- Page Editor

- Widget Editor
- New Portal
- Get Help

Different Portals:
- Employee Center
- Service Portal
- Anonymous Report Center
- Knowledge Portal
- SP Configuration
- Walk-up

47. UI Policy

Overview:

- Behavior of form elements
- Conditions
- Actions
- Scope
- Order of Execution

Service Catalog UI Policy:

- For specific Catalog Item
- Catalog Item Variable/Variable Set
- Limited UI policy functionality
- Requested Item/Catalog Task
- Priority Order

UI Policy Form:

- Table
- Short description
- Order
- When to apply
- Script
- UI Policy Action
- Applies to
- Catalog Item or Variable Set

UI Policy

UI Policy Scripts:

- Client-Side API
- Run scripts
- Execute if true
- Execute if false

Use Cases:

- Show/Hide Field
- Making a Field Mandatory
- Setting a Field as Read-Only
- Show Alert Message
- Clear Variable Value

48. UI Actions

Overview:
- Custom Actions/Buttons
- Extend and Customize
- Enhancing User Experience
- Streamlining Processes
- Increasing Adoption

UI action controls:
- Form Button
- Context menu item
- Related Link
- Banner Button
- Bottom of a list.
- List context menu
- Action choice list

UI Action Form:
- Name
- Table
- Order
- Action name
- Show insert
- Show update

UI Actions

- Client
- Form button
- Form context menu
- Form link
- List banner button
- List bottom button

Restricting UI actions:

- Restrict UI Actions
- Visibility Rule
- Exclude rule
- Include rule

Override for Extended Table:

- Remove UI Action
- Same Action Name
- Script
- Add Condition

49. Business Rules

Overview:
- Automate processes
- Server-side Script
- Server-side Conditions
- Database Operation
- Scoped Applications

How business rules work:
- Before
- After
- A sync
- Display
- Insert
- Update
- Query
- Delete

Business Rule Form:
- Accessible from
- Advanced
- When
- Order
- Filter Conditions

Business Rules

- Role Condition
- Abort action

Global variables:

- Current
- previous
- g_scratchpad
- gs

Technical Best Practices:

- Know When to Run Business Rules
- Use Conditions
- Keep Code in Functions
- Prevent Recursive Business Rules
- Double-Check Critical Input
- Use Script Includes Instead of Global Business Rules

50. Data Policy

Overview:

- Data Consistency
- Similar to UI policies
- Rules
- Scope
- Role

Data Policy Rules:

- Server-side Logic
- Field Attributes
- Conditions
- Actions

Data Policy Form:

- Table
- Inherit
- Reverse if false
- Apply to import sets
- Apply to SOAP

Data Policy vs. UI Policy:

- Execute based on field values
- Execute on form save/submit/update

Data Policy

- Execute on form field value change
- Set field Visibility attribute
- Set field attributes with no scripting
- Execute scripts for advanced logic

Best Practices:
- Clearly Define Data Requirements
- Prioritize Data Policies
- Keep Policies Simple and Specific
- Test Thoroughly
- Consider Performance Impacts
- Leverage Scoped Applications
- Use as UI Policy on client

Glossary

Glossary

AJAX	(Asynchronous JavaScript And XML)
API	(Application Program Interface)
APM	(Application Portfolio Management)
AWS	(Amazon Web Service)
CAD	(Certified Application Developer)
CAS	(Certified Application Specialist)
CAS-PA	(Certified Application Specialist – Performance Analytics)
CCS	(Catalog Client Scripts)
CEs	(Underpinning Contracts)
CIs	(Configuration Items)
CIS	(Certified Implementation Specialist)
CMDB	(Configuration Management Database)
COE	(Center of Excellence)
CPG	(Cloud Provisioning and Governance)
CR	(Change Request)
CRUD	(Create, Read, Update, Delete)
CSA	(Certified System Administrator)
CSM	(Customer Services Management)
CSS	(Custom Style Sheets)
Disco	(Discovery)
EM	(Event Management)
FMA	(Multi-Factor Authentication)
FSM	(Field Service Management)
FTPS	(Secure File Transfer Protocol)
GRC	(Governance Risk and Compliance)
HAM	(Hardware Asset Management)
HRSD	(HR Service Delivery)

Glossary

HTML	(Hyper Text Markup Language)
IaaS	(Infrastructure-as-a-Service)
IRE	(Identification and Reconciliation Engine)
ITAM	(IT Assets Management)
ITBM	(IT Business Management)
ITIL	(IT Infrastructure Library)
ITOM	(IT Operations Management)
ITSM	(IT Services Management)
JDBC	(Java Database Connectivity)
JSON	(JavaScript Object Notation)
KB	(Knowledge Base)
KCS	(Knowledge-Centered Service)
KPIs	(Key Performance Indicators)
LDAP	(Lightweight Directory Access Protocol)
MAM	(Mobile Application Management)
MDM	(Mobile Device Management)
OLA	(Operations Level Agreement)
OOAD	(Object Oriented Analysis and Design)
OOB	(Out of the Box)
PaaS	(Platforms-as-a-Service)
PL/SQL	(Procedural Language for SQL)
PPM	(Project Portfolio Management)
PPM	(Project Portfolio Management)
RC	(Risk & Compliance)
REST	(RESTful)
SaaS	(Software-as-a-Service)
SAM	(Software Asset Management)
SAML	(Security Assertion Markup Language)

SCCM	(System Center Configuration Manager)
SDLC	(Software Development Life Cycle)
SecOps	(Security Operations)
SIR	(Security Incident Response)
SLA	(Service Level Agreement)
SM	(Service Mapping)
SNPI	(ServiceNow Platform Implementation)
SOAP	(Simple object access protocol)
SP	(Service Provider)
SQL	(Structured Query Language)
SSO	(Single Sign-On)
UAT	(User Acceptance Testing)
UI	(User Interface)
URIs	(Uniform Resource Identifiers)
URL	(Uniform Resource Locators)
UX	(User Experience)
VA	(Virtual Agents)
VMs	(Virtual Machines)
VR	(Vulnerability Response)
VRM	(Vendor Risk Management)
W3C	(World Wide Web Consortium)
WebDAV	(Web Distributed Authoring and Versioning)
WSDL	(Web Service Description Language)
XML	(Extensible Markup Language)
XSLT	(Extensible Stylesheet Language Transformations)

Made in the USA
Columbia, SC
21 November 2024

47245779R00075